In honor of:

_____

_____

_____

Forever Remembered

A single life touches many hearts—and together
we gather to honor someone truly beloved. As a
treasured guest, friend, and family member, please
share your thoughts, feelings, and memories in
these pages. Write from your heart. Let it say
whatever it needs to say, in any way you'd like.
Your words will forever be cherished. And know
that your presence here means so much.

I CARRY YOUR HEART WITH ME...

E. E. Cummings

To love abundantly is
to live abundantly,
and to love forever is
to live forever.

Henry Drummond

I CAN LOOK INTO THE WORLD
AND SEE YOU IN EVERY ACT OF LOVE.
WHERE ONCE YOU WERE ONE,
YOU ARE NOW MANY.

Molly Fumia

There are some who
bring a light so great
to the world that even
after they have gone,
the light remains.

_____

Unknown

MY FRIENDS HAVE MADE THE STORY OF MY LIFE.

———————————

Helen Keller

...a life spent loving...
is a life well spent.

Suzanne Clothier

LIFE STARTS WITH LOVE AND ENDS WITH LOVE.

————————————

Santosh Kalwar

If I should ever leave you whom I love
To go along the Silent Way, grieve not.
Nor speak of me with tears, but laugh and talk
Of me as if I were beside you there.

_____

Isla Paschal Richardson

MEMORIES NEED TO BE SHARED.

———————————

Lois Lowry

And I will light a candle for you
to shatter all the darkness
and bless the times we knew.

Paul Alexander

IN THE END, IT'S NOT THE YEARS IN YOUR LIFE
THAT COUNT, IT'S THE LIFE IN YOUR YEARS.

Unknown

We remember best
what we love most.

_____

Warren Goddard

BLESSED INFLUENCE OF ONE TRUE
LOVING HUMAN SOUL ON ANOTHER!

———————————

George Eliot

Those whom we have loved
never really leave us. They live
on forever in our hearts,
and cast their radiant light
onto our every shadow.

———————————————————

Sylvana Rossetti

WE ARE NEVER ALONE IN OUR GRIEF...

———————————

Unknown

The ones we love are
always in our hearts.
_____

Proverb

I WILL NEVER FORGET YOU EVEN FOR AN INTERVAL...

———————————

Izumi Shikibu

Memories are our
greatest inheritance.

Peter Hamill

THERE ARE NO GOODBYES FOR US.

Mahatma Gandhi

Thank you for coming into
my life and giving me joy,
thank you for loving me and
receiving my love in return.
Thank you for the memories
I will cherish forever.

_____

Nicholas Sparks

I LEAVE YOU LOVE.

—————————————

Mary McLeod Bethune

In one of the stars I shall be living.
In one of them I shall be laughing.
And so it will be as if all the stars
will be laughing when you look at
the sky at night.

Antoine de Saint-Exupéry

THE ONLY LASTING BEAUTY IS
THE BEAUTY OF THE HEART.

———————————

Rumi

Looking back over a lifetime,
you see that love was the
answer to everything.

_____

Ray Bradbury

LIFE IS A SHARED EXPERIENCE.

_____

Unknown

Through love, through friendship,
a heart lives more than one life...

_____

Anaïs Nin

I AM PART OF ALL THAT I HAVE MET.

Alfred, Lord Tennyson

The effect of one
good-hearted person
is incalculable.

_____

Óscar Arias

AMONG LIFE'S BEST GIFTS ARE THE
FRIENDS WHO KNOW AND CARE ABOUT US.

———————————

Gayle Larson

...thank you, forever and sincerely...

Elizabeth Gilbert

THE MEMORIES I VALUE MOST,
I DON'T EVER SEE THEM FADING.

Kazuo Ishiguro

I remember them always
and everywhere...

_____

Anna Akhmatova

TO LIVE IN HEARTS WE LEAVE BEHIND IS NOT TO DIE.

————————————

Thomas Campbell

Love is the emblem
of eternity: it confounds
all notion of time;
effaces all memory of
a beginning, all fear
of an end...

Germaine de Staël

NOTHING IS EVER REALLY LOST TO US
AS LONG AS WE REMEMBER IT.

L. M. Montgomery

...that place in the heart
   that holds the measure of
   your history, the joy and
   the grief, the laughter
   and the tears, the magic
   and the wonder; all the
   ingredients that add up to
   the story of a life well lived.

Lilli Jolgren Day

ALL WHO HAVE BEEN TOUCHED BY BEAUTY ARE
TOUCHED BY SORROW AT ITS PASSING.

———————————

Louise Cordana

What the heart remembers
most are moments shared.

Elizabeth Browne

I EMBRACE YOU WITH ALL MY HEART.

Albert Camus

With special thanks to the entire Compendium family.

CREDITS:

Written & Compiled by: Miriam Hathaway

Designed by: Jill Labieniec

Edited by: Kristin Eade

ISBN: 978-1-946873-36-1

1st printing. Printed in China with soy and metallic inks.